Glad Sounds

Eric A. Thorn

Words Edition

Autumn House

Books by Eric A. Thorn include:

Understanding Copyright: A Practical Guide	(Jay Books)
A Question of Copyright	(Jay Books)
Let's Sing and Make Music	(Jay Books)
The Effective Bookstall	(Jay Books)
Resource Material for The Effective Bookstall	(Jay Books)
The Chosen Few (with Roger Jones)	(Christian Music Ministries)
Tell me the Stories of Jesus (with Roger Jones)	(McCrimmon)
Wildlife and Environment Anthology (Editor)	(Effective Publishing)

Acknowledgement: Some of the items in this book have appeared in other collections, including *The Chosen Few* (Christian Music Ministries).

ISBN: 1-873796-41-2

Also Available

Sound Recording: An audio recording of songs in this collection is available on cassette. This is ideal for both your leisure listening and also as an excellent resource for learning the various pieces. *Music Edition:* Provides full music including guitar chords. These items are available from your usual dealer.

Autumn House
Alma Park, Grantham, Lincolnshire, NG31 9SL, United Kingdom

Introduction

Every new generation boasts its own unique popular styles of music. Despite (or, perhaps, *in spite of*) that fact, there is no doubt that music and singing has the effect of linking together people of all ages. Many of the pieces in this book certainly go a long way towards reinforcing this fact: they have been used and enjoyed in times of family worship when all age-groups have been represented.

For convenience of use, all of the pieces that were specially written for children or children and adults together have been placed at the beginning (numbers 1-18). But this is by no means an arbitrary situation: a reasonable number of the other pieces have been, and will doubtless continue to be, thoroughly enjoyed by young people. We strongly encourage you to try every song! A few have been given a choice of two tunes in the music edition, and where this is the case we encourage you to try out both.

A good many of these songs were specially written for particular events or special services. These had to meet the criteria, therefore, of being relatively easy to play, sing and enjoy. In practice, the tunes of virtually all the items were picked up very quickly, especially when each person had his or her own copy of the words edition. Listening to the audio cassette also proved to be a great learning resource.

In turn, the same criteria was applied when selecting items for inclusion in this book, plus the additional aspects that (1), each item should be considered as suitable for use by congregations of all denominations, and (2), all those written primarily for children should be considered suitable for general use in first and middle schools, junior church, holiday clubs and so on. Various churches, schools and choirs have been involved with trying out the items, and to them we proffer our thanks. Only those pieces that received top recommendations were finally included.

It is our prayer that you will enjoy playing and singing these hymns and songs as much as we have enjoyed writing them. Make a joyful noise! Improvise by adding some percussion and/or other instruments (for some helpful hints please refer to *Let's Sing and Make Music* published by Jay Books). Guitar chords are included in the music edition.

We are always delighted to hear from anybody with any comments about our hymns and songs, and we also like to receive reports from those who have used any of our pieces for particular events. Also, we are encouraged when we are invited to write something for any school, church or other organisation. Our postal address is:

c/o Autumn House, Alma Park, Grantham, Lincolnshire, NG31 9SL

Eric A. Thorn
Roger and Julia Stepney
Little Common, Lent 1994

1: At Bethlehem

At Bethlehem
you came down to us,
born for all of us,
Son of God.
Born in a stable cold and dark,
laid in a manger for an ark,
born for the world, for ev'ry part,
Jesus Christ.

At Nazareth
you grew up for us,
born for all of us,
Son of Man.
Learnt as a carpenter your trade,
worked with a plane and worked with lathe,
prized all the things that you had made,
Jesus Christ.

At Calvary
you were hung for us,
bore our sins for us,
Son of God.
Rising again you saved us all,
pouring new life upon us all,
so that your Name we now enthrall,
Jesus Christ.

2: Creation Around Me

I see the flowers,
I see the trees,
And in the meadow
    I see daises.
And if God so clothes the daises,
How much more will he love me!
Yes, if God so clothes the daises,
How much more must he love me!

I see the sparrows,
I see the clouds,
And in the sunlight
    I see swallows.
And if God so feeds the swallows,
How much more will he love me!
Yes, if God so feeds the swallows,
How much more must he love me!

3: Great World

Isn't this a great world?
Such a great world,
    and God's the one who made it!
Sun and moon and stars so bright,
God made day and God made night.
Fish in the sea; birds in the air:
God's great love is ev'rywhere.

Isn't this a great world?
Such a great world,
    and God's own son died for it!
Jesus hung upon a tree;
We may join God's family.
Trust in God's word; pray to the Lord;
God's great love is here for all.

4a: Forms of Harvest

There's a rustling on the common
as the leaves float in the breeze;
There's a gorgeous recreation
as we play among the trees:

There are conkers, there are acorns,
which we gather by the score;
There are blackberries and apples,
and we'd love to gather more!

There is coal and there is charcoal,
there is gas and there is wood;
There's electric and there's oi-l;
All these fu-els are so good!

There's a duckling in the water,
and a swan all clean and white;
There's a goldfish swimming after,
in the autumn warm sunlight.

All of these are forms of harvest
that we all tend to forget;
But our God will not ignore us,
though we put him to the test:

There's a greatness in the harvest,
which is more than we can know,
planned by God who reigns in glory
from the heavens to below.

4b: Forms of Harvest

There's a rustling on the common
as the leaves float in the breeze;
There's a gorgeous recreation
as we play among the trees:
There are conkers, there are acorns,
which we gather by the score;
There are blackberries and apples,
and we'd love to gather more!

There is coal and there is charcoal,
there is gas and there is wood;
There's electric and there's oi-l;
All these fu-els are so good!
There's a duckling in the water,
and a swan all clean and white;
There's a goldfish swimming after
in the autumn warm sunlight.

All of these are forms of harvest
that we all tend to forget;
But our God will not ignore us,
though we put him to the test:
There's a greatness in the harvest,
which is more than we can know,
planned by God who reigns in glory
from the heavens to below.

5: Fun

Look at all the golden corn
ripened by the burning sun,
Dancing in the breeze so cool,
Watching it is fun,
Watching it is fun.

Look at all the apples there
ripened by the glowing sun,
Lots of fruit for us to share,
Sharing it is fun,
Sharing it is fun.

Look at all the Dandelions
lazing in the summer sun;
See the bumble bees ride past
having so much fun,
having so much fun.

Look at all the grass so green,
ripened by the glowing sun.
We can play upon the grass:
Playing there is fun,
Playing there is fun!

6: Go! Tell!

One dark night in Beth'lem
a baby boy was born
in a stone cold stable,
born for all the world.

> *Go, tell it to your neighbours,*
> *over the fence and in their house.*
> *Go, tell it to your neighbours:*
> *Jesus Christ is born!*

Shepherds on the mountains
were watching all their sheep.
Angels came and told them
of a new-born King.

> *Go, tell it on the hillsides,*
> *over the fields and everywhere.*
> *Go, tell it on the hillsides,*
> *Jesus Christ is King!*

Jesus Christ in Beth'lem
was born for all the world
in a stone cold stable,
born to save us all.

> *Go, tell it to the whole world,*
> *over the seas to every land.*
> *Go, tell it to the whole world:*
> *Jesus came to save!*

7: God's Love is so Big and Strong

Sometimes I feel I'm all alone,
and that's not very nice;
But Jesus isn't far away:
he comes to break the ice.

Chorus: *The wonderful thing about God's love
is it's so big and strong;
The wonderful thing about God's love
is it's so big and strong
that even little ones like me
can know that we belong,
yes, the wonderful thing about God's love
is it's so big and strong.*

Sometimes things don't go well at school,
and everything's bad news;
But Jesus cheers me up again:
he takes away those blues.   *[chorus]*

Sometimes I don't get on at home,
and everything goes wrong;
But Jesus comforts me, and then
I sing a happy song.   *[chorus]*

Sometimes my friends don't have the time
to come around for tea;
But Jesus is my special friend:
he's always time for me.

*The wonderful thing about God's love
is it's so big and strong;
The wonderful thing about God's love
is it's so big and strong
that everybody in the world
may know that they belong,
yes, the wonderful thing about God's love
is it's so big and strong.*

8: I Like Reading

I like reading in my Bible
all the stories Jesus told;
They are really quite exciting,
somehow never do grow old.
Like Walt Disney's fairy stories,
Bible stories are unique:
They appeal to ev'rybody,
help to make their lives complete.

I was reading in my Bible
how a lamb just wandered off,
but the shepherd went and found him,
placed him back within the flock.
Then I read that a nice lady
lost a sentimental thing;
How she searched until she found it,
then she had a jolly sing!

I was reading in my Bible
how a chap just left his home,
never 'phoned or wrote a letter
'til somehow he was alone.
Then he said that he was sorry,
made his father cry for joy:
roasted calf was served at table,
in the honour of his boy!

I was reading in my Bible
Jesus died to save our souls;
We must follow him and trust him,
he who gave his life for us.
There's lots more within the Bible,
you may read it for yourself;
You will find it so exciting,
you won't keep it to yourself!

9: Knocking at My Door

Jesus comes knocking at my door,
Jesus comes knocking at my door;
He's so patient for my answer,
he just keeps knocking at my door.

Jesus would like to come inside,
Jesus would like to come inside;
He's so willing to just love me,
he just keeps waiting to come in.

Jesus would like to change my life,
Jesus would like to change my life;
He's so patient for my answer,
he just keeps knocking at my door.

10: My Friend Jesus

Jesus is my friend,
he's with me ev'ryday.
I know that he is near me
at home, at school, at play.

Jesus is my friend,
he's with me ev'ry night.
I know that he is near me
when I switch off the light.

Jesus is my friend,
he's with me ev'ry week.
I know that he is near me
and guards me when I sleep.

Jesus is my friend,
he's with me all the time;
If you're a friend of Jesus,
then you're a friend of mine.

11: Praises Sing

Praises sing to Jesus,
Praises sing to Jesus,
Praises sing to Jesus
who died upon a tree.

Praise to our Lord Jesus,
Praise to our Lord Jesus,
Praise to our Lord Jesus,
who died to set us free.

Praise to God, the Father,
Praise to God, the Father,
Praise to God, the Father,
the Son, and Holy Ghost.

Praise to our Lord Jesus,
Praise to our Lord Jesus,
Praise to our Lord Jesus,
who died that we may live.

12: My Mum Says

I like stomping in the puddles,
I like skipping in the rain.
My Mum says it's rather naughty,
My Mum says that I'm a pain!
My shoes get so very muddy,
My coat gets all dirty, too.
My Mum says she doesn't like me
doing what my best friends do!

I like climbing up the Oak tree,
I like sliding down again.
My Mum says I'm up to mischief,
My Mum says that I'm a pain.
My clothes get so many holes in,
and they get so many tears.
My Mum says she doesn't like to
keep on doing my repairs!

I like helping with the housework,
I like helping Mum to clean.
My Mum says that I'm a good-en,
My Mum says I'm very keen.
Though sometimes I do jobs badly,
things just don't go right for me,
My Mum says it doesn't matter:
God loves me, and so does she!

Phew!
My Mum says that she still loves me
just the way that God made me.
Yes! Just the way that God made me.

13: Our Harvest Day is Over

Our Harvest Day is over
for yet another year.
The gifts we've brought to Jesus
are now before us here.
Before we go, again we raise
our thanks to God above
for all that he provides us with
from his great hand of love.

We thank God for providing
fresh air for us to breathe.
Thirst-quenching water, also,
to us he does bequeath.
Fresh fruit and daily bread as well
are gifts from God above;
tinned foods, and eggs, and poultry come
from our great God of love.

Our clothes and health come also
from God's all-gracious hand;
our happiness is something
which he again has planned.
But something more important still
comes to us through God's love —
eternal life through his dear son:
all praise to God above!
All praise to God above!

14: Ring the Bells

Ring the bells, light the lamps,
Jesus Christ is born,
ring the bells, light the lamps,
God as man is born.

> *Children sing and clap and cheer,*
> *for the Saviour now is here.*
> *Children sing and clap and cheer,*
> *God as babe is here!*

Ring the bells, light the lamps,
God has come to earth,
ring the bells, light the lamps,
bringing us new birth.

> *Children sing and clap and cheer,*
> *for the Saviour now is here.*
> *Children sing and clap and cheer,*
> *God as boy is here!*

Ring the bells, light the lamps,
let creation sing:
ring the bells, light the lamps,
praises to their King.

> *Gather round and clap and cheer,*
> *for the Saviour now is here.*
> *Gather round and clap and cheer,*
> *Christ our King is here!*

15: Some Days

Some days are not the best ones;
just nothing goes quite right.
No-one seems to understand,
and I just get uptight:
I do things I don't mean to do,
and say things I don't mean.
And ev'rybody says, "Cheer up,
things aren't quite what they seem".

They say if you're a Christian
you have an easy time:
Jesus takes all hurt away
and then you get on fine.
But in my case it's not like that!
As far as I can see
the Christian life is stern and hard,
not full of mirth and glee.

Sometimes I've done things which I
have known it wrong to do,
though I've tried to stop myself
and think the matter through.
The fact is that I find it hard
however much I try.
And when I think about my day
it often makes me cry.

But when my tantrum's over
I think through what I've done.
Letting down my friends, and God,
from dawn to setting sun.
And when I think about myself
in shame, on bended knee,
then Jesus is forgiving, and
I find he still loves me.

16: Thank You

Thank you for the sunshine, Lord, and
    thank you for the rain.
Thank you for the monsoon time, and
    for the hurricane.
Thank you, thank you, Lord,
thank you, thank you, Lord.

Thank you for the breezy wind, and
    for all times of drought.
'Though the winter's sometimes bad it
    shows that you're about.
Thank you, thank you, Lord,
thank you, thank you, Lord.

Thank you for my family, and
    thank you for my friends.
Thank you for my teachers, Lord, their
    patience never ends!
Thank you, thank you, Lord,
thank you, thank you, Lord.

17: The Good Samaritan

Once a man set out to go
down the road to Jericho.
On the way he was attacked
by a thief, who hurt his back,
left him lying helpless there
in a state of sore despair.

Then a Levite wandered by,
saw this man all fit to die.
Crossed on to the other side,
passed by with a quick, long stride.
Didn't want to get involved:
soon his problem would be solved.

Not long after came a priest,
saw this man just like a beast;
dripping blood and looking bad,
in his situation sad.
Priest, too, passed the trav'ller by,
left him lonesome, fit to die.

Then an outcast came along,
heard the man's sad, pleading song.
Stopped and bound his wounds up well,
took him to a good hotel.
Paid the bill, and bid his friend
stay, 'til he was on the mend.

Jesus tells us, "Don't pass by,
leaving fellow men to die:
in the name of God above
just stretch out a hand of love.
Ev'ry little task, you see,
is performed as unto me".

18: What a Great Day!

What a great day it is
    despite the weather;
What a great day it is
    to praise the Lord!
What a great day it is
    although it's cloudy:
It's a great day for us
    to praise the Lord!

It's a great day today,
    for Jesus loves us;
It's a great day today,
    we love him too!
It's a great day today,
    for he forgives us:
It's a great joy when we
    just praise the Lord!

What a great day it is
    to sing God's praises;
What a great day it is
    to read his word.
What a great day it is
    to speak to him, and
what a great day it is
    to praise the Lord!

Yes,
what a great day it is
to praise the Lord!

19: Apocalypse

The world is ending: hear the trumpets,
Jesus comes to claim his own.
The world is ending: hear the trumpets,
Jesus comes to claim his own.
Songs of angels,
Hallelujah!
Songs of angels,
Hallelujah!
Fill the earth as God comes down.

The world is ending: hark, the judgement
of the living and the dead.
The world is ending: hark, the judgement
of the living and the dead.
Songs of angels,
Hallelujah!
Songs of angels,
Hallelujah!
Fill the heav'ns as Jesus reigns.

The world is ending: praise King Jesus,
kneel before him everyone!
The world is ending: praise King Jesus,
kneel before him everyone!
Praise King Jesus,
Hallelujah!
Praise King Jesus,
Hallelujah!
Jesus reigns for evermore!

20: Confidence

The Lord shall be your confidence,
the Lord shall be your guide;
the Lord shall be your sturdy bridge
o'er waters deep and wide.
His strength alone your staff and shield,
his might alone your pow'r;
with God all things are possible
if you trust him this hour.

Not through your human strength and hope
could you achieve a thing:
but through the Spirit of our Lord
if you have faith in him.
The Lord shall prove his promises
can never, never fall;
for he shall work his miracles
throughout your life in all.

The Lord shall be your counsellor,
your one true friend indeed.
The Lord shall be your comforter
in times when grace you need.
His word shall light the path you tread,
his hand clasped in your own.
Your power and your glory is
of God, of God alone.

21: Easter Hymn

Hark how all the new bells ring,
chiming glory to the King,
peace in hearts of men on earth:
theirs is now a glad rebirth.

> *Chorus:*
> *Jesus Christ has won the day:*
> *he is risen, come what may.*
> *He has won the victor's crown,*
> *Lucifer is feeling down!*

Three long days and nights have passed
since he to the cross was cast.
Three days' prison was the gain
of the only Son of Man.

Counted dead, but just today
who has rolled the stone away?
Jesus Christ, the Son of Man,
is fulfilling God's great plan.

Hark how all the new bells ring,
chiming glory to the King,
peace in hearts of men on earth:
theirs is now a glad rebirth.

22: Eucharist

Jesus our Head you gave us your life,
broken to meet our need.
Showed us the way to end all our strife,
if we would intercede.
So as your body here we eat,
for you have shown us how,
may hunger end within our souls,
Bread of real life, just now.

Jesus our Lord you gave us a well
of living water pure.
Showed us the way to end all our thirst,
gave us a lasting cure.
So as your blood we now drink all,
for you have shown us how,
may thirst be quenched within our souls,
Blood of real life, just now.

Jesus our King you gave us the strength,
through your commissioned meal,
to share your love around all the world,
as you have love for all:
Here at your feast we all partake,
for you have shown us how;
May we not hunger any more:
Fill our souls richly — now!

23: Go Nationwide

Go forth to Africa, go nationwide,
Jesus is sending us for whom he died.
Is Jesus calling you to Africa
to spread his love and peace nationwide there?

Go forth to India, and to Brazil,
Jesus is sending us to help and heal.
Is Jesus calling you to lands afar
to spread his love and truth nationwide there?

Go forth to far Hong Kong, go nationwide,
Jesus is calling us for whom he died.
Is Jesus calling you to go abroad
to spread his love and peace
              round the whole world?

"Go forth to all the world,"
           is Christ's command;
in faith and prayer they go, that joyful band
who, by devotion in their lives, can share
good news of Christ our Lord globalwide there.

24: Healing

Jesus, healer from on high,
left upon a cross to die.
Ev'ry day we seek anew
by our faith, new life in you.

Lepers at a distance stayed,
"Pity us", was what they prayed.
Christ said, "Go", and they were cured
of the sickness they endured.

Here's a great Centurion
with a dying servant man.
Sent for Christ to say the word;
instant healing then occurred.

Woman with a haemorrhage
touched his clothing at its edge.
Jesus said, "Your faith in me
makes you well eternally".

Blind man, at the city gate,
called for Jesus Christ to wait.
"Don't pass by, but heal my blight".
Jesus said, "Receive your sight"!

Jairus' daughter on her bed
breathed her last, and lay quite dead.
Jesus said, "Her eyes are closed",
took her hand, and she arose.

Christ can heal our souls as well,
save us from eternal Hell.
For he takes our sin away
when we ask him in to stay.

Great Physician, each new day
hear us, as we humbly pray;
Glad that hearts and minds are healed
through our faith in God revealed.

25: Penitence

Christ triumphant, risen Lord,
King of kings, by all adored.
Sadly we've rejected you
and your making all things new.

We have lived in our own way,
and we've let you down each day.
In your mercy and your grace,
rid us all of this disgrace.

We have turned from faith in you,
not believing what you do.
In your mercy help us to
live the gospel through and through.

We have served ourselves alone,
swept aside our heav'nly home.
Now we come in humble fuss:
in your mercy, Lord, save us.

Lift our thoughts to things above;
let us wallow in your love.
Clothe us with your spirit's power,
help us serve you hour by hour.

26: I'll Sing of Him

I'll sing of Jesus Christ, his mercy crowns my days.
He fills my life with love, and hears my praise.
I'll sing of Christ, for I've faith in the son of God
who died for me, and bought me with his blood.
He died for me, and bought me with his blood.

I'll sing of Jesus Christ when, kneeling at his feet,
he fills my mind with love, and grace so sweet.
My song of Christ over-rides what else may betide;
I'll sing of grace that keeps me by God's side.
I'll sing of grace that keeps me by his side.

I'll sing of Jesus Christ, as I go on my way
he lights my path with love, and hears me pray.
And when my soul does arrive at God's heaven fair,
I'll join the praise that is perpetual there.
I'll join the praise that is perpetual there.

27: Intercessory Hymn

Lord, within this land of ou-rs
there are those who've never heard
of the love that comes from Jesus
if we take him at his word;
so we pray for those around us,
all around our country too:
may they find that through your Spirit
they can claim true love in you.

Lord, we pray for friends and neighbours,
may they come to call you *"Friend"*,
may they find your understanding
something they can comprehend.
Lord, we pray for those around us,
mums and dads and children too:
may they find that through your Spirit
they can claim true love in you.

Lord, within our congregation
there are those who need your hand,
so we pray for one another:
for this is your true command.
Lord, we plead that you will aid us
as your work we seek to do:
may we find that through your Spirit
we can claim true love in you.

28: Jesus Came

It was just because of evil men
that Jesus came to earth;
he came two thousand years ago
with poor and lowly birth.
He lived a life of toil and strife,
and died to give mankind new life.
He came down
because of sinful men.

Chorus:
King Jesus lives for ever:
he lives within my heart,
and he helps me in my labours,
yes, he helps in every part.
He gives me strength to do his will
and makes his presence oh so real.
He loves me
and lives within my heart!

It was just because he loves the world
that God sent down his son.
He wants to see all sin dispelled,
and then the vict'ry won.
God let his son die on a tree:
a ransom made for you and me.
Jesus Christ,
he died to take our sin.

It was just because of love for all
that Jesus rose again.
And if we on his name will call
his message is quite plain:
he'll enter any pleading soul,
and make that soul for ever whole.
Jesus Christ,
he died to save us all.

29: Jesus is Coming Again

Jesus, you were born at Beth'lem,
with a manger for a bed.
All the shelter you were offered
was a musty cattle shed.
But, O Lord, we praise you truly
that you came on earth to live.
And, O Lord, again you're coming:
what a wondrous truth this is!

Jesus, you were then rejected
by all those who disbelieved.
Hear their cry, "Release Barabbas",
thinking that they've been deceived.
But, O Lord, we praise you truly
for we know that yet you live.
And, O Lord, again you're coming:
what a wondrous truth this is!

Jesus, you were followed wholly
when you walked upon this earth
healing, blessing, and yet teaching
all mankind your true rebirth.
And, O Lord, we praise you truly
that you came on earth to live.
And, O Lord, again you're coming:
what a wondrous truth this is!

Jesus, you have died to save us,
you were taken in our place.
Nailed upon that cross of Calv'ry
you were hung in sore disgrace.
But, O Lord, we praise you truly
for we know that yet you live.
And, O Lord, again you're coming:
what a wondrous truth this is!

Jesus, you have ris'n in glory,
reigning by your Father's side.
Through our trusting you we pray that
we one day shall there abide.
Lord, we thank you for the knowledge
that you will return again.
And, O Lord, we praise you truly
that you've won an endless reign!

30: Jesus, My Lord

solo or unison:	I met you at the cross,
harmony:	Jesus my Lord:
solo or unison:	I heard you from that cross:
harmony:	Jesus my Lord,
solo or unison:	my name you called.
harmony:	Jesus my Lord.
solo or unison:	Asked me to follow you all of my days, asked me for evermore your name to praise.
harmony:	Jesus my Lord, Jesus my Lord.

solo or unison:	I saw you on the cross
harmony:	dying for me,
solo or unison:	I put you on that cross:
harmony:	but your one plea:
solo or unison:	My name you called.
harmony:	Jesus my Lord.
solo or unison:	Would I now follow you all of my days, and would I evermore your great name praise?
harmony:	Jesus my Lord, Jesus my Lord.

solo or unison:	Jesus, my Lord and King,
harmony:	Saviour of all,
solo or unison:	Jesus the King of kings,
harmony:	you heard my call:
solo or unison:	My name you called.
harmony:	Jesus my Lord.
solo or unison:	That I would follow you all of my days, and that for evermore your name I'd praise.
harmony:	Jesus my Lord, Jesus my Lord.

31: John 3:16

God so loved the world, he gave us
Jesus Christ, his only heir;
And whoever trusts in Jesus
will not perish into Hell.
For each one who trusts in Jesus
everlasting life may claim;
Yes! Each one who trusts in Jesus,
everlasting life may claim.

In love beyond understanding
Jesus died to take our place:
On the cross, that first Good Friday,
he was hung in sore disgrace.
But he rose again to glory,
where he has an endless reign;
And each one who trusts in Jesus
everlasting life may claim.

32: Let's Remember

Come, let all of us remember,
near the end of each December,
how God sent his only son to earth.
Through the joys and through the splendours,
whilst we gaze into the embers,
let's recall God's humble, human birth.

Come, let all of us remember
how the star with bright endeavour
led men to the place of Jesus' birth.
Over hillsides, down through valleys,
to the land once ruled by David:
Bethlehem, the place of Jesus' birth.

Come, let all of us remember
frankincense and myrrh for ever.
Even gold was brought to God's own son.
Through these gifts, and through the giving,
and the lives that we are living,
let's recall the gift of God's own son.

Come, let all of us remember
Jesus laid within a manger
with the frightened cattle standing by.
Soon this child, serene and tender —
bonny baby, happy gurgling —
we will send to Calvary to die.

Come, let all of us remember,
near the end of each December,
how God sent his only son to earth.
Through the joys and through the splendours,
whilst we gaze into the embers,
let's recall God's humble, human birth.

33: Saints

From near and far
we worship in this place.
Combined as one;
a family through grace.
    Like saints of old
        we sing of him
    who died to rid
        the world of sin.

We are your saints,
we come before you now.
For as your saints
to you we humbly bow.
    Like saints of old
        we worship Christ
    who died to give
        the world new life.

Across the globe
the saints will pray for us.
And we in faith
remember them, and trust
    that all will meet
        on that great day
    when trumpets gleam
        in bright array.

When glory comes
and saints go marching in,
the trumpets sound
our turn to join their line.
    With saints of old
        we'll meet our Lord,
    and worship God
        with one accord.

34: Song of Friendship

Lord, we seek your special blessing
on this couple here today;
help them overcome all sorrow
they may meet upon life's way.
As together they go forward
may their world be so unique
that, with problems solved together,
they may find their lives complete.

Lord, we see this happy couple
smiling now before our eyes,
may their love be something special,
love be that which never dies.
In their home may they be joyful,
guided only by God's hand,
walking side by side for ever
in the steps which he has planned.

Bless this couple, Lord, with children,
that they may be ever young.
Mould them in your hand together,
thus your will for them be done.
Keep their love for ever faithful
to each other and to you:
for whom God has joined together
even death cannot undo.

35: The Offering of Life

The off'ring of life for a living sacrifice
    is not an easy thing,
but Jesus died to give my soul new life
    and now he is my King.

> *Will you give your life to the King of kings?*
> *Will you offer him service true?*
> *Will you praise and worship now the*
>   *holy Son of God*
> *who died for me and you?*

The pledging of life to the one and only Lord
    is not an easy thing,
but Jesus rose and now he calls us all
    to put our faith in him.

> *Will you give your life to the King of kings?*
> *Will you offer him service true?*
> *Will you praise and worship now the*
>   *holy Son of God*
> *who died for me and you?*

36: Through the Church of Jesus

Through the Church of Jesus
we are joined as one,
united by the Father,
the Spirit, and the Son.
Through the Church of Jesus
we are fully blessed;
the peace that Jesus gives us
is our perfect rest.

Jesus is the one to
whom we turn each day;
we ask him for his pardon
if we have gone astray.
Jesus is the one who
helps us on our way:
he guides and he protects us
each and ev'ry day.

Through the love of Jesus
we are born again;
we look toward the coming
of Jesus' endless reign.
And the love of Jesus
is for ever true:
the love that Jesus gives us
is for ever new.

37: Upside Down

Jesus is King of all the world,
and his truth is growing all unfurled.
It's a truth that can save,
It's a truth that we crave,
and it's turning the world upside down.

The truth Jesus brings is one of love
and it comes from Heaven up above.
Love our neighbours, we must,
and our enemies; just
love is turning the world upside down.

The truth Jesus brings is for us all,
that we must before the Master fall.
For if we trust in him
he will lead us from sin:
Truth is turning the world upside down.

The truth Jesus brings is what we plead;
and it comes from Jesus in our need.
In this truth we find zest,
and yet we find our rest:
It's what's turning the world upside down.

38: We Bring Our Lives

O Jesus, we have promised
that we will follow you,
and practise your example
in ev'rything we do.
We do not understand, Lord,
all the commands you give,
yet you are always with us
as Christian lives we live.

O Jesus, you have told us
to take this bread and wine
in memory of your death, Lord,
and also as a sign.
The bread: your broken body
hung up upon a tree.
The wine: your blood shed for us
at darkest Calvary.

O Jesus, you have shown us
that we aren't wasting time:
the promise of your coming
is in this bread and wine.
And also at this supper
we do as we believe:
we bring our lives, to offer
ourselves, as we receive.

39: Unite us in Love, Peace and Joy

Unite us in love,
Christ's body on earth,
and let our love prove
Christ offers new birth.

Unite us in peace,
Christ's body on earth,
and let our peace show
Christ offers new birth.

Unite us in joy,
Christ's body on earth,
and let our joy tell
Christ offers new birth.

Unite us on earth,
and let our lives show
through love, peace and joy,
the Christ whom we know.

Index of First Lines

(Titles are also listed where these differ from the first line)

Subject Index
(These are suggestions only, provided as a guide)